Poems for Heartwork

What Does Your Heart Say?

Poems for Heartwork
by
Richard Wehrman

Merlinwood Books • East Bloomfield, New York

Dedicated to you
who struggle and have found the way
to Awaken.

ISBN: 978-1-7344648-1-8

Merlinwood Books
PO. Box 146
East Bloomfield, NY 14443

www.richardwehrman.com
richard@richardwehrman.com

. . . .

For more information about The Heartwork Institute,
visit www.awakentheheart.org

If God came
down to Earth,
and walked among us,
how could I tell
His hand
from Yours?

HEARTWORK, a therapeutic process originated by
Dale Goldstein, is a practice of letting go with awareness
into the truth of one's being in the moment. A synthesis
of Eastern meditative approaches and Western psychology
and philosophy, it uses awareness as the primary vehicle to
see into the source of one's problems. As a spiritual path,
the work is to inquire deeply into one's experience in the
moment to come to know one's True Nature.

❁

This short collection of poems was inspired by the Author's
direct experience of the Heartwork process. The poems
were previously published in a small limited edition for a
Heartwork Intensive held in Austin, Texas in 2004.

CONTENTS ❀

SOMETIMES

Sometimes
there is a time
when pretending,
and the cheery face,
just won't hold anymore.

And the body begins to come apart.

The old straps
holding you together burst,

one   after   another.

And what you were,
who you are,
just simply falls apart.

It's like standing
in the waters of a pond,
and slowly sliding down
below those bright autumn leaves.

To a place,
to a pain,
to a scream,
to a no longer holding anything,

any   thing.

Because
nothing you hold,
nothing you try to make,
to create,
will hold together.

And in that
darkest place,

when all is given up—
All is let go, because
there is

NO WAY TO MAKE IT WORK

Sometimes,

when you are exhausted,
when there is no
strength for
even sobbing

sometimes,

you may find
yourself delivered

onto the shore
and sunrise

of a new day.

TOTALLY SAFE

I always thought
the fear would leave
when walls were thick and high enough.

When money was in vast supply—
and anything I needed
could be bought.

That when the gates were shut
no enemies, no creditors,
no angry men or women,

No bearers of
you should do this, you should do that,
could get inside.

My guns and arrows
would all be the latest type;
would utterly destroy
all enemies before me.

My best defense—complete defense.
But such safety comes at great expense.
How many old and young have smashed
themselves upon that rock?

So I spent my gold, all that I owned
to build these fortress walls.
Now here I sit
In a vast and heavy prison
of iron and stone and steel;
Unable to go out, unable to let in.

And what I do each day
from history and from habit—
is shoot down, destroy,

any trying to get near.

～

Now sitting in
this empty space, I remember:

> My need to be protected
> was just my need to feel held.
> To be totally included—
> in no way left out.

So wonderful to know
your whole life's striving
brings you to the place you fear the most.

And you might be here for a very long time.

～

But like a pendulum
the swing begins again.
From agedness to youth

I will return
by a different road:
from protectedness towards all I fear;

to abandon and lay down
with every step
some expensive weapon of intricate design,

removing bit by bit
whatever shield or armor
stands between my naked breast

and the bare point
of what I think will kill me,

pull me down or cast me out.

Until at last I see that
ALL ARE WELCOME.

No one, no thing, can be refused.
No visitor can call to whom I would say no.

Fear is gone;
kneeling I unpack a flag
I've carried all my life—
Folded tight and hidden from the sun.

Unfurled and wide upon the wind
three letters blaze the antidote to death:

I won't turn back.

My flag flies
YES!

THE WALL

This morning
I woke to the wall.

And the wall was
clear and stretched and tight
and I was Alice at the Looking Glass—

looking at the beauty of the sun
and flowers and the rain-shine
glowing on the other side.

But this wall held me in—
no matter where I pushed;
its membrane held me tight.

And the wall was...
    and the wall was...

Everything that didn't happen right.
Every time I hoped
    and hope was crushed.
Every time I loved
    and love was lost.
Every time I gave myself
    and pain and loss were given back.
Every time I trusted
    and my trust came back betrayed.

And the wall said:

This is the way it will always be...
    this is the way it will always be...

And my heart broke from this wall.
I cried and cried—
For it would not let me breathe:

All in here is stale and harsh and used—
the exhausting heat
of living in one room.

And so one simple way
to end this story is to say:
Upon the floor,
I spied a knife—a tiny, puny thing.
But then, perhaps it was a pen,
and not a knife.
And like this one I write with now—

It pushed its point
against the wall, as I push
now against this paper—
pushed it hard and stretching.
And writing faster, harder,
now excited and insistent and unwilling to remain
here one more day:

the point—I think—

The point
is going
through!

WE ARE SAILORS

We are sailors
on a strange dark sea,
Shoving our boarded boats
from shore and sand
into riotous nights
of wind and crashing
thunder.

When all sane men
(could we but be)
at home well covered
in dry warm
beds lie lee.

But here our driven-ness
and our call,
all soaked and thrown and tossed—
Tumbling,
brothered by fear,
lamped by longing—

Find we are

Rowing,
rowing fiercely
toward the darkest center
of the storm.

WHAT WE WANT

We tell ourselves
we want the safety
of the homey walls,
security and surety
against the thousand
thousand things.

But what we really want,
above all else,
is to die our death at Sea—
Fighting for our life
with every strength
our bodies be.

To hurl
with our last breath
into Great Emptiness
our soul—

As far,
as deep,
as it will go.

THIS WAY HOME

O precious one,
Some days you are gone far away
and I feel so totally alone.
I call and call,
but we cannot hear each other.
Our eyes meet
yet no one is at home.

I know this place—
this dry grey desert where nothing grows.
I've wandered there myself
for years upon endless years.

But amazingly, one day someone must have loved me.
For they left a little rope winding through
the drifting dunes:
I picked it up—
and someone pulled me forward;
following my feet I came at last upon this green
and fragrant paradise.

Today—O precious one,
while you slept so soundly,
I too have left a rope
in the dry and quiet desert.
There is so little left to do—
it's not that hard at all:

Just bend down
and pick it up.
Just hold it in your warm
and beautiful
hands.

MONDAY MORNING

Did I ever tell you how great you are?

Did I ever say:
    "It's just so wonderful you're here"?

Have I ever hugged you
    when you thought that you were bad?

Do you know your face is like the Sun to me?
    That when I see you,
        my whole body feels warm,
            and safe and loved?

You know,
    in all the world of what you do
        and how you do it,
            It's — just — fine.

You always do it "right"
    even when you think
        you did it wrong!

If I said,
    and I do say it now–
        That you are Joy beyond belief,

You are such Happiness
    that I can barely stand it—
        that just to be around you makes me dance,
            and jump, unable to be still—

Would you believe me?

Go now.
    Look in the mirror,
        and tell me what you see:

"Hello my Friend! It's Us in here.
Come out and play away the day with Me."

You think I'm just a voice inside your head,
or a poem written from a friend—
But really,
I am just your own Love speaking—
shouting out:

"I'm so glad you're here!
So glad that you've come Home!"

SOMEONE'S PUT A FILE IN
MY LOAF OF BREAD

I've lived too long
in this city
of right and wrong.
Every friend I knew here
has been imprisoned, tortured
or cruelly put to death.
The jailer's reasons
all made perfect sense:
not one could argue with their proofs
or with the truth of what they said.
It's just what's left
is that all my friends
are dead.
And so—though it makes no earthly sense—
I must leave this home where I grew up.
By killing all I loved,
they cut the chains that held me here.
And now the Crazy One with
his wide bright eyes
waits for me outside the gate
of the southern wall.
He's cut the bars
and freed the stones around them;
Everything I need
is packed,
safe inside my heart.
Tonight on the full moon
two lunatics will flee—
away to the lush, ripe oasis of Zanzibar—
far from this vast grey crumbling city,
the city
of the Sane.

MY HEART IS POURING

Oh weary One,
tired and exhausted
from years of tight defending:
Come now—lean into my arms.
You have stumbled
into the tavern
where you took
your very first drink.
Tonight,
all you have to do
is raise your glass
before me—
For my heart's love
is pouring freely—
And you, dear friend,
may drink
without
restraint.

LOVE FOR SALE

I have become
a merchant of Love,
selling piecemeal from
the trunk of my car.
Hundreds pass me by each day,
so afraid of my ragged joy.
But for those who risk
my wild-eyed strangeness,
I have a bargain
they could never guess:
Their stopping was my payment,
and in return
I fill their hands
with rubies and with emeralds,
sapphires dripping
like blue fire—
They cry "Enough!"
yet still I pour
the jewels of my heart—
falling through their fingers,
gathering like
spring's blossoms,
drifted
around their feet.

STEALING FROM HAFIZ

Today Hafiz has whispered
a secret in my ear:

> At every meeting,
> we are always saying to each other:
> *Love me*

We rarely will admit this.
Almost never will we say it straight out loud.
But look inside, you know it's true.

> Everywhere in the world
> hearts are seeking hearts.

Now here come your old friends;
the ones you smile at every day from habit—

> Why not take a chance,
> and let them have for free
> the gift they've always wished for—

their Heart's Desire, unspoken,
just like yours.

DREAMING

Losing the thread
is so easy.
All of a sudden
you're way down the road of
what might be—
thinking, this could be a good idea,
maybe I'll live here,
fall in love, get married.

Then it's like waking up.

You the sleepwalker:
cold, outdoors without jacket or pants
standing in the thin snow,
no shoes on your feet.
The wind is sharp,
the bare trees bright.

And you're wondering
where you've been, and

how the hell
you got here.

THE NIGHT PRAYER

Full of fear in the night,
I asked God for strength—
He said, "You have always
been fearless!"

Feeling so empty and alone
I asked God to fill me—
He said, "You have always
been full."

Feeling so separate and adrift,
I asked God to hold me—
He said, "Dear one, since time began,
you have never been out
of my arms."

And so, in peace at last,
I slept.

STEP FORWARD

We don't want
to think it can be
so easy:

That one thin sharp blade
can cut through
ten-thousand years
of rope;

That though you have been
bound and frozen
for all of time—

When warmth arrives
all coldness melts away.

Incomprehensible,
incredulous!
We have to drop what binds us;

We are the ones to step forward,
to relax our clutched
and gripping hands.

TIPPING POINT

All these years
building up this house
that by the end must be
completely broken down—

each piece carted away,
each stone replaced, just so—
timbers replanted in the earth
and watered, glass pulverized to sand.

So, standing on the tipping point,
looking back to what
you have become through so
much labor, so much pain—

and gazing forward
to the slowly shrinking edifice,
a sugar cube dissolving in the rain—

What can you say? What can you do?
But shake his hand goodbye,
say, "Thanks for all the dedication and
hard work, but now I've got to go."

Like Milarepa, grateful now to Marpa—
joyfully, with growing vigor
and excitement,

not to mention wonder—
pulling down and blessing
each round stone.

MIDAS

What a simple secret!
Like Midas,
every touch is gold!
But here,
the gold is Life!
And every
place you light upon
explodes—
blossoms burst
from dead dry wood,
Each touch,
the treasure of your
One True Love,
touching back
at you.

GENIE

Once outside the bottle
there is no going back.

Oh, the days will come when
you'll beg for your old home—
for the darkness, the cramped

closeness, with the walls up
tight where you can feel them,
holding you in.

But you can't go back.
The being you are now has grown
too large, too vast.

And though you feel the fear
so fiercely with each new
giant step you take, now
the little one is gone—

and all the tiny aches and pains,
the imaginings of great disaster
have died like water on the witch,

like smoke now rising in a boil
to greatness unimagined.

Towering, billowing into
the broad blue sky, the words
our unplugged ears have so long
strained to hear

roll loud as thunder
crashing down the universe:

Free! FREE!
FREE AT LAST!

NO ONE LEFT BEHIND

Nothing is abandoned.

When the ship sails
the open heart can leave
nothing behind.

Who could bear it?
Mother her child—
Lover the beloved?

Any part of who we are,
Any god or goddess
who taught us what it is to be:

All those wearing masks
of terror or delight—
Pain or suffering gifted
over years of unwavering devotion,
standing all at the gate,
pressing from the dock,
silently calling, waving their goodbyes—

Oh! Their and my own tears
streaming: Break the barrier!
Let them all aboard.

This ark sails to a new land
and none of who I am
or what we all can be
will be left on any shore
behind, adrift, abandoned.

Into this new world
we will set foot
fully whole,
and free!

JOURNEY

For years
I thought God
would show up
in a flash and dazzle—

Decking me out
in gold and silks,
gifting me with palaces and jewels,
where I would live out
a kingly life of ease.

But these days,
though God looms large
on my horizon—
it is often misty and most days
hard to see.

Our movement
towards each other
comes tightly measured—
in single steps,
in difficult and long lived days.

And our final greeting
may be less
a joyous celebration
full of gold and glitter—

than Each,
falling exhausted,
into the others'
Arms.

THE ONLY ONE LEFT

All fear,
all revelation,
all beauty and amazement,
arise from your own Mind.

You are the source of it all.

You stare at vaporous
black squiggles upon a white page,
and insight arises.

From where?

You hear a cacophony of sounds,
no different than wind in the trees,
or leaves tumbling over the ground,
and you bow in gratitude
to your teacher.

Where is this teacher?

You think it all comes
from somewhere else.

Listen!
Where is it all actually occurring?

I don't mean to sound angry—
but this is Me, shaking You:

Right now these tumbling letters
are rattling around inside your head
and you think it's me talking to you,

when really it is your own Mystery—
Alive and fully present,
creating me, these words,
and everything else you see.

Wake up! See this one who reads,
this one who writes.

In this search of a thousand years,
we've freed the usual suspects—
and as unlikely as it seemed
in the beginning,

You are the only
One left.

WETNESS

God
seeps into
everything—

Why worry if
"This one's got it right" or
"That one's got it wrong"?

Whatever touches water
becomes wet
through and through.

There is no way
to get this wrong.

Whenever you speak
God emerges—

standing suddenly
in your old clothes,

sitting now
in your favorite
chair.

THE CURRENT OF LOVE

You are trying to make
this thing with your head,
when it is your Heart
that wants to speak.

You're afraid that love
will lead you into twisted
paths and confusion.

Oh, Be Confused!

Twist and turn faster and faster,
until this Great Confusion becomes
your Dance of Ecstasy!

Abandon your so-called sanity.
That knuckle-boned grip
is strangling the last bit of your Life.

Open your heart to the current of love.
It's there in you.
You know it.

But continually you seek
the desert rocks of your mind.
Step out of your dry nest
into the wet falling rain;

Let it carry you easily
over all obstacles down to the Sea—
To the one who has waited
for ten-thousand years,

arms always open,
calling again and again your

own sweet name.

SERVANT

This one has
held it all together for you.
He's worked so hard,
indeed into a frenzy;

his manic activity and
strange paranoid devices
had convinced you he was quite insane—

a total maniac without a license,
driving a ten-ton truck.
Careening and bouncing off walls,
he's built fortresses and castles,
made war with all your neighbors,
and filled the rooms with treasure,
food and beautiful women.

But in the end he's done it all for you.

Left alone in an empty house,
what could he do
but build a cargo cult
in your own honor?

Now it has become a sub-division,
a city-state of personhood
built all the way to your front door.
In his last bit of craziness,

he's lowered the drawbridge,
and though he doesn't
know it yet himself, he waits

expectantly, excitedly
for your great,
triumphant
return.

YOU ARE

One day
everything wakes up.

The glass you have
been filling for so long,
finally is full.

You raise the blinds, and
the sun rises over the Eastern hill.

There is no mystery here at all.

You are the One you sought.

Overnight a spring
began flowing from a crack
in the dry earth—

Now there is water everywhere, and
everything dry and brittle has become
luscious and green—

and Who You Really Are
has become the source
of all life,

Yourself.

HOME

The worn shoes
rest on the doorway,
leather cracked and stained.

A thousand miles of wandering
has molded them to the shape
of your feet.

But now
you've stepped inside,
removed your socks,
and feel the yellow sunlight,
warm on the polished wood floor.

Wherever you walk now,
you are in your own body.

And whether on green grass
or sharp gravel,

Nothing stands
between you and
the whole wide world.

THE RAIN

The rain passed by
and the evening sun broke through,

blazing the just-turned oaks,
and lit up all our faces, gold,
too bright to look upon:
myself and all my friends.

Those in this life
that found their way
to the same shore,

where we passed a line of life
around and through us—
tying our selves together
with the cords we did not know,
until very near the end,
were the woven strands of braided love.

And we could have cried,
and did,
because there we were:
each for the other, each for ourselves;

we had risked all,
and gained it,
and gave it back again to each other,
into the blazing glow
of each beloved face—

as the rain grew light and quieted,
as the golden light fell upon us all,

as the storm broke,
gave us grace,
and moved on.

WHAT I REALLY WANT

All I want to do
is to give you reassurance.

All I want to say
is that everything's OK.

All I want,
for all of us,
is to crest the next green hill,

to hold each other tightly,
to speak into
the setting sun:

"Look.
We did it.
We made it Home, at last."

www.ingramcontent.com/pod-product-compliance
Lightning Source LLC
Chambersburg PA
CBHW032105040426
42449CB00007B/1195